TESTIMONIALS

"Shut Up, Stop Whining was the first Winget book I picked up and I felt a connection like never before with an author. Filled with straight talk and straight answers, Larry's honest approach is a brutally refreshing retreat from all of the esoteric blather that the so-called gurus preach. Take personal responsibility for your place in the world and stand up and be a man (or a woman.) It's time to get a life!"

Tommy Zarzecki, Publisher, PlanetZman.com
The Last great Bastion for Real Men

. . . .

"There should be school courses – Winget 101 – starting in grade school.
The USA would start getting back to what it used to be."
Steve Watson

. . . .

"You freaking rock, Larry!! Thanks for inspiring so many of us."
Patrick Healey

. . . .

"Great stuff, Larry. You tell it like it is . . . what people need to hear instead of what they would like to hear."
Paul Barker

. . . .

"He's overwrought with righteous awesomesauce."
Michael Wilson

SHUT UP, STOP WHINING & GET A LIFE

A Kick-Butt Approach to a Better Life

from

SmarterComics™

Larry Winget

Illustrated by Shane Clester

Adapted by Cullen Bunn

Executive Editor
Corey Michael Blake

Creative Director
Nathan Brown

Comic book cover design based on original artwork by Susan Olinsky.

A Round Table Companies Production
www.roundtablepress.com

INTRODUCTION

Have you heard stuff like this before:

"JUST HAVE A POSITIVE ATTITUDE AND EVERYTHING IN YOUR LIFE WILL BE OKAY."

"AS LONG AS YOU FEEL REALLY GOOD ABOUT YOUR-SELF, EVERYTHING WILL BE TERRIFIC!"

"THE KEY TO SUCCESS IS TO BE YOURSELF."

Of course you have! All over the world you can find people telling you that sort of drivel from books, stages, and the airwaves. All of the gurus of the personal development industry talk about how important it is to be yourself, have a positive attitude, and to feel good about yourself. What a happy load of crap!

My message is not like that. I don't care if you are being yourself or if you feel good about yourself. I don't even care if you have a negative attitude. I'm not into cute little sayings that will have very little effect on achieving success. So welcome to my world!

People buy into those ideas because they sound good, but they end up with very few tangible results. They then become frustrated and disillusioned, and end up abandoning their pursuit of being more, doing more and having more. They become complacent and settle for less than they have to. In some cases they become bitter about the whole process. Sound familiar to you?

HERE IS THE PROBLEM: NO ONE EVER TOLD THEM YOUR LIFE IS YOUR OWN FAULT!

That is the place we all have to get to before we can start making real progress toward achieving success. In fact, I'll go so far as to say that no real success can be achieved until you accept the fact that your life is your own fault. You are responsible. Your thoughts, words and actions created the life you are living. Even on the outside chance that something horrible happened to you that you had nothing to do with, how you react to that event is still your fault. What you do about it is your fault. It's always your fault. Once you understand that and take responsibility for your life at every level you will begin to achieve success.

That stance is what makes my approach different from others in the personal development industry. (That plus the earrings and the shirts and the boots!) I don't believe in blaming or making excuses, and I won't listen to your whining, complaining or pointing the finger of blame anywhere other than your own face. You may think that is a mean, heartless approach but I assure you it isn't. It is an approach that is rooted in caring and truth and reality. I care enough to tell you the truth so you will face reality.

That's why I wrote the book, *Shut Up, Stop Whining & Get A Life* and why I am so excited that you are reading this new illustrated version of my bestselling book. This is the book that started it all for me and set me apart from all of the warm and fuzzy pat-you-on-the-head-and-tell-you-it's-all-going-to-be-okay motivational books on the market. The success of this hardcore self-help book led me to write four other bestsellers: *It's Called Work For A Reason; You're Broke Because You Want To Be; People Are Idiots and I Can Prove It;* and *Your Kids Are Your Own Fault.*

My goal in writing this book was not to make you feel better. My goal is to remind you to go to the only place in the world where you can lay blame: the mirror. And it will give you a simple, easy to follow plan that can point you in the direction of success, happiness and prosperity. The book is divided into three parts:

SHUT UP! Chances are you are talking too much and need to listen. Or as my Dad used to tell me: "You're broadcasting when you ought to be tuned in."

STOP WHINING. Wallowing in your problems doesn't fix your problems so stop complaining, blaming, griping, bitching, moaning and groaning and take responsibility for your life.

GET A LIFE. Create the life you want to have by living by design and not by default. Make a decision, create a plan and then go to work to make that plan come to life. Simple? Of course! Easy? Not always. Worth it? Absolutely. Now read the book and change your life!

By the way, thanks to the good people of SmarterComics and Writers of the Round Table, and to Shane Clester for the terrific illustrations. They were all great to deal with on every level and the cool factor for what they produced is off the charts!

Larry Winget

SHUT UP, STOP WHINING & GET A LIFE

A Kick-Butt Approach to a Better Life

from

SmarterComics™

LISTEN TO OTHERS—ESPECIALLY YOUR LOVED ONES.

MOST PEOPLE THINK COMMUNICATION IS ABOUT TALKING. THAT IS ONLY A SMALL PART OF IT.

LISTENING IS THE BIGGEST PART. BECOME VERY GOOD AT IT WITH THOSE YOU LOVE.

LISTEN TO YOUR CUSTOMERS, WHETHER THEY ARE CALLED PATIENTS, CLIENTS, CO-WORKERS, OR THE AUDIENCE.

THE BEST WAY TO SERVE THEM WELL IS BY HEARING WHAT THEY'RE SAYING.

LISTEN TO THOSE WHO KNOW MORE THAN YOU DO.

SPEND TIME WITH THOSE WHO ARE DOING BETTER THAN YOU. FIGURE OUT WHAT THEY ARE DOING, THEN GO DO IT YOURSELF.

DUPLICATE THEIR ACTIONS AND YOUR CHANCES OF DUPLICATING THEIR SUCCESS IMPROVES.

LISTEN TO THE EXPERTS—GREAT TEACHERS, SPEAKERS, AND PHILOSOPHERS. AND SINCE SO MANY BOOKS AND PRESENTATIONS ARE AVAILABLE ON CD OR DIGITAL DOWNLOAD, YOUR BEST TEACHERS CAN COME TO YOU ON YOUR SCHEDULE.

BUT WE ARE A NATION OF WHINERS AND BLAMERS—A SOCIETY OF VICTIMS. IT AMAZES ME THAT PEOPLE CAN BLAME EVERYONE EXCEPT THEMSELVES FOR THEIR PROBLEMS.

SMOKERS BLAME CIGARETTE COMPANIES FOR THEIR POOR HEALTH.

KOFF KOFF

FAT PEOPLE BLAME FAST FOOD RESTAURANTS OR THEIR GENES FOR THEIR WEIGHT.

I JUST DON'T KNOW WHY MY METABOLISM ISN'T WORKING LIKE IT USED TO.

MNOM MNOM

THE TRUTH IS, BAD THINGS HAPPEN. THOSE THINGS MAY OR MAY NOT BE YOUR FAULT, BUT HOW YOU REACT TO THEM IS DEFINITELY YOUR FAULT.

YOU CANNOT FOCUS ON SOLUTIONS WHEN YOU ARE WHINING ABOUT THE PROBLEM.

@#*!!

REMEMBER, YOU CAN ONLY CHOOSE ONE THING TO DO. YOU CAN WHINE OR YOU CAN CREATE A PLAN THAT MOVES YOU TOWARDS THE LIFE YOU WANT.

HOPEFULLY, YOU'RE AS SICK OF YOUR "LESS THAN IDEAL" LIFE AS I AM OF HEARING YOU WHINE ABOUT IT. ARE YOU READY TO CHANGE? ARE YOU READY TO DO SOMETHING ABOUT IT?

I DOUBT IT.

THAT MAY SOUND CRUEL, BUT I'VE HEARD IT ALL BEFORE. YOU'VE PROBABLY SAID IT BEFORE.

YOU'VE HEARD THE PHRASE "READY, WILLING, AND ABLE" BEFORE, HAVEN'T YOU?

EVERYONE IS READY TO DO MORE AND HAVE GREATER SUCCESS. AT LEAST THEY THINK THEY ARE OR SAY THEY ARE.

MOST PEOPLE ARE ABLE TO DO MORE. WHETHER YOU FACE CHALLENGES THAT ARE MENTAL, FINANCIAL, OR PHYSICAL, YOU ARE STILL ABLE TO DO MORE.

THE PROBLEM IS, FEW PEOPLE ARE WILLING TO DO MORE IN ORDER TO HAVE WHAT THEY WANT IN LIFE.

SO LET'S TALK ABOUT LIVING BY DESIGN INSTEAD OF BY DEFAULT.

YOU'VE CREATED EVERYTHING THAT HAS EVER HAPPENED IN YOUR LIFE, BOTH GOOD AND BAD.

WHAT YOU THINK ABOUT, TALK ABOUT, AND DO SOMETHING ABOUT IS WHAT COMES ABOUT. YOUR THOUGHTS, WORDS, AND ACTIONS EITHER MOVE YOU CLOSER TO WHERE YOU WANT OR FURTHER AWAY FROM WHERE YOU WANT TO BE.

LET'S FACE IT. YOU KNOW YOU NEED A CHANGE. BUT KNOWING IS NOT ENOUGH.

KNOWLEDGE IS NOT POWER. IT IS THE IMPLEMENTATION THAT IS POWER.

CHANGE YOUR WORDS. WHAT YOU SAY PROGRAMS WHAT HAPPENS. YOUR WORDS ATTRACT TO YOU EITHER THE LIFE YOU WANT OR THE LIFE YOU DON'T WANT. SAYING THINGS LIKE—

I'M NOT GOOD ENOUGH FOR HER...

--ONLY PERPETUATES THE FACT THAT YOU'RE TOO MUCH OF A LOSER TO ASK OUT THAT GIRL WHO CAUGHT YOUR EYE.

INSTEAD OF TALKING ABOUT THE THINGS YOU DON'T WANT TO HAPPEN, START EACH DAY PROCLAIMING WHAT YOU WANT TO HAPPEN.

THAT KIND OF AFFIRMATION IS POWERFUL, BUT REMEMBER THAT AFFIRMATION WITHOUT IMPLEMENTATION IS SELF-DELUSION.

POP!

CHANGE YOUR THINKING. WHEN YOU THINK DIFFERENTLY OF YOURSELF AND YOUR ABILITIES TO ACCOMPLISH YOUR DESIRES, YOU WILL THINK DIFFERENTLY ABOUT THE REST OF THE WORLD.

YOU'VE ALSO GOT TO CHANGE YOUR ACTIONS.

WHENEVER YOU ARE ABOUT TO TAKE ACTION, ASK YOURSELF—

IS THIS ACTION IN ALIGNMENT WITH THE HIGHEST VISION OF MYSELF?

IF YOU WANT SOMETHING DIFFERENT, YOU HAVE TO CHANGE THE WAY YOU DO THINGS.

REMEMBER HOW YOU DID THINGS YESTERDAY? DON'T DO THEM THAT WAY TODAY. DON'T THINK OF THEM THE SAME WAY. DON'T TALK ABOUT THEM THE WAY YOU DID.

EVERY LITTLE THING YOU THINK, SAY, AND DO HAS A MAJOR IMPACT ON THE OUTCOME OF YOUR LIFE.

MASTER THESE AND THE WORLD BELONGS TO YOU.

THOUGHTS ARE CREATIVE. WORDS ARE CREATIVE. ACTIONS ARE CREATIVE. THESE ARE THE THREE CREATIVE FORCES OF THE UNIVERSE.

SPEND SOME TIME DETERMINING EXACTLY WHAT YOU WANT OUT OF LIFE.

WHAT DO YOU WANT TO ACCOMPLISH? HOW DO YOU WANT TO DRESS? WHAT KIND OF CAR DO YOU WANT TO DRIVE? WHERE WOULD YOU LIKE TO TRAVEL? WHAT KIND OF RELATIONSHIP DO YOU WANT WITH YOUR FAMILY?

WRITE DOWN A DESCRIPTION OF THE LIFE YOU WANT. I BET IT LOOKS SIGNIFICANTLY DIFFERENT THAN YOUR CURRENT LIFE.

A WORD OF CAUTION: THE LIFE YOU WANT COMES AT A PRICE, JUST LIKE EVERYTHING ELSE.

WANT TO BE FIT AND TRIM? THE PRICE IS DECREASED CALORIES AND INCREASED EXERCISE.

WANT TO BE RICH? YOU HAVE TO WORK HARDER, LONGER, OR SMARTER—POSSIBLY ALL THREE.

WANT TO BE HAPPY? YOU HAVE TO GIVE UP EVERYTHING THAT MAKES YOU UNHAPPY.

THE REALITY OF LIFE IS THAT YOU WILL PAY A PRICE, ONE WAY OR ANOTHER. ONE PRICE GIVES YOU EXACTLY WHAT YOU WANT. THE OTHER GIVES YOU EXACTLY WHAT YOU DON'T WANT.

THE GOOD NEWS IS THAT THE LIFE YOU WANT COMES CHEAPER THAN THE LIFE YOU DON'T WANT. THE LIFE YOU DON'T WANT MAKES YOU MISERABLE, UNHEALTHY, AND BROKE. THAT PRICE IS SIMPLY TOO HIGH!

FIRST—AND THIS ONE WILL BLOW YOUR MIND—ATTITUDE IS **NOT** EVERYTHING.

A POSITIVE ATTITUDE IS GREAT, BUT IT WILL NOT KEEP ONE BAD THING FROM HAPPENING TO YOU.

YOU CAN BE POSITIVE AND STILL END UP POSITIVELY WRONG AND POSITIVELY MISERABLE!

ATTITUDE IS IMPORTANT, NOT BECAUSE IT PREVENTS BAD THINGS FROM HAPPENING, BUT BECAUSE IT HELPS YOU DEAL WITH WHAT HAPPENS TO YOU.

BUT ATTITUDE ALONE WILL CHANGE NOTHING. THOUGHT CHANGES THINGS. WORDS CHANGE THINGS. EFFORT CHANGES THINGS. ACTION CHANGES THINGS.

AND GUESS WHAT...SOMETIMES IT'S GOOD TO HAVE A BAD ATTITUDE.

BEING NEGATIVE CAN SERVE YOU WELL. SOMETIMES YOU NEED TO GET MAD—MAD AT YOURSELF FOR BEING THE PERSON YOU ARE...MAD AT THE WAY YOU ARE BEHAVING...MAD AT HOW YOU ARE RUNNING YOUR BUSINESS...

IN ORDER TO MAKE POSITIVE CHANGES IN YOUR LIFE, YOU MUST FIRST GET NEGATIVE ABOUT YOUR LIFE. FEELING GOOD DOES NOT CREATE CHANGE. FEELING UNCOMFORTABLE CREATES CHANGE.

IF YOU DON'T FEEL AT LEAST A LITTLE UNCOMFORTABLE ABOUT HOW YOUR LIFE HAS TURNED OUT, YOU'LL NEVER CHANGE.

I WANT YOU TO FEEL UNCOMFORTABLE. WHY? BECAUSE I WANT YOU TO CHANGE. I WANT YOU TO DISCOVER YOUR BEST SELF AND GO FOR IT.

MOTIVATION THAT MAKES YOU FEEL GOOD ABOUT YOURSELF WILL NOT CHANGE YOUR LIFE.

YOU CAN DO JUST ABOUT ANYTHING YOU WANT TO DO. BUT YOU WILL NOT DO IT BY FEELING GOOD ABOUT YOURSELF.

BUT IT STILL TAKES MORE THAN JUST FEELING GOOD ABOUT YOURSELF AND KNOWING YOU CAN DO WHATEVER YOU WANT. IT TAKES BELIEVING!

THAT BELIEF WILL PROPEL YOU TO AMAZING HEIGHTS.

BUT REMEMBER, YOU HAVE TO A HAVE A PLAN, TOO.

MOTIVATION WITHOUT A PLAN IS STUPID.

MOTIVATION TYPICALLY MEANS SOME OUTSIDE FORCE WILL INSPIRE YOU TO FEEL GOOD ENOUGH ABOUT YOURSELF SO YOU WILL DO ANYTHING YOUR LITTLE HEART DESIRES.

THE TRUTH IS, IN ORDER TO DO ANYTHING YOUR HEART DESIRES, YOU MUST KNOW YOU CAN DO ANYTHING—AND THEN TAKE ACTION ON IT!

TAKE SOME RISKS. HAVE COURAGE. JUST DO WHAT YOU NEED TO DO AND CONTINUE DOING IT UNTIL YOU GET WHAT YOU WANT.

GRAND OPENING

COFFEE KLATCH

HERE ARE A FEW MORE MOTIVATIONAL MYTHS THAT CAN KEEP YOU FROM REACHING YOUR GOALS.

"YOU CAN BE WHATEVER YOU WANT TO BE."

TEENY magazine

WHAT SEXY AIN'T!

How To Be A Better

YOU KNOW BETTER THAN THIS. YOU CAN BECOME WHATEVER YOU HAVE THE TALENT FOR, THE POTENTIAL TO BECOME, AND ARE WILLING TO DEDICATE THE TIME AND EFFORT INTO BECOMING.

"YOU CAN HAVE WHATEVER YOU WANT TO HAVE."

YOU CAN HAVE WHAT YOU DESERVE, AND WHATEVER YOU TAKE ACTION TOWARD ACHIEVING. YOU DON'T GET WHAT YOU WANT. YOU GET WHAT YOU TAKE ACTION ON.

"YOU BECOME WHAT YOU THINK ABOUT."

HA HA HA HA HA HA HA

IF THAT WERE TRUE, MOST TEENAGE BOYS WOULD BE GIRLS!

THE TRUTH IS, YOU BECOME WHAT YOU THINK ABOUT, TALK ABOUT, AND DO SOMETHING ABOUT.

"THERE ARE NO PROBLEMS, ONLY OPPORTUNITIES."

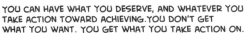

GLUB GLUB

SOMETIMES, A PROBLEM IS JUST A PROBLEM. EVERY PROBLEM CAN TEACH US A VALUABLE LESSON, BUT IT STILL NEEDS TO BE CALLED A PROBLEM AND DEALT WITH LIKE A PROBLEM.

"GIVE 110%"

DANGER

YOU CANNOT GIVE 110 PERCENT. IT IS IMPOSSIBLE. ONE-HUNDRED PERCENT IS ALL THERE IS. I'LL GRANT YOU THAT YOU CAN DO MORE THAN YOU THINK YOU CAN. YOU ALWAYS HAVE MORE TO GIVE. BUT YOU CANNOT GIVE MORE THAN THERE IS.

MOST PEOPLE, BY THE WAY, SEEM TO BE COMFORTABLE OPERATING AT ABOUT 60%.

WHAT YOU BELIEVE DETERMINES WHAT YOU HAVE, HOW MUCH MONEY YOU MAKE, HOW HEALTHY YOU ARE, AND HOW SUCCESSFUL YOU ARE.

I CAN PROBABLY TELL WHAT YOU BELIEVE...

...BY LOOKING AT YOUR BANK ACCOUNT...

...YOUR CAR...

...OR EVEN YOUR SHOES...

I CAN TELL WHAT YOU BELIEVE BY LOOKING AT YOUR RELATIONSHIPS...HOW YOU SPEND YOUR FREE TIME... OR WHAT TV SHOWS YOU WATCH...

JERRY! JERRY! JERRY!

YOUR BELIEFS ALWAYS SHOW UP IN YOUR LIFE. WITHOUT EXCEPTION, YOU ALWAYS MANIFEST YOUR BELIEF SYSTEM. TAKE A LOOK AT YOUR LIFE AND DETERMINE WHAT BELIEF YOU HAVE THAT HAS CREATED AND SUPPORTED THE RESULTS. IF YOU AREN'T HAPPY WITH THE RESULTS, CHANGE YOUR BELIEFS.

MY GUESS IS YOU ARE NOT HAVING AS MUCH FUN AS YOU SHOULD HAVE AND CERTAINLY NOT AS MUCH FUN AS YOU COULD HAVE.

YOU PROBABLY DON'T HAVE THAT MUCH FUN AT WORK, BUT YOU TOLERATE IT.

YOU MIGHT NOT HAVE A LOT OF FUN HANGING OUT WITH YOUR FRIENDS, BUT REPLACING THEM SEEMS LIKE A LOT OF TROUBLE.

YOU MIGHT NOT ENJOY THE WAY YOU DRESS OR THE WAY YOU LOOK.

YOU NEED TO CHANGE YOUR WAY OF THINKING WHEN IT COMES TO ENJOYING LIFE!

AN ABSENCE OF ENJOYMENT INDICATES THE PRESENCE OF FRUSTRATION. FRUSTRATION LEADS TO NEGATIVITY.

NEGATIVITY IN YOUR LIFE MEANS YOU WILL REACT NEGATIVELY TO EVERYONE AND EVERYTHING.

BUT YOU CAN SUBMIT TO TOTAL ENJOYMENT AND MAKE MONEY, HAVE BETTER RELATIONSHIPS, BE MORE SUCCESSFUL, AND HAVE MORE FUN THAN EVER BEFORE!

BOTTOM LINE—YOU DON'T HAVE TO DO THINGS YOU DO NOT ENJOY. REALLY.

DON'T ENJOY YOUR JOB? EITHER QUIT AND FIND SOMETHING YOU DO ENJOY OR LEARN TO ENJOY THE JOB YOU HAVE. BUT DON'T QUIT UNLESS YOU HAVE SOMETHING ELSE LINED UP!

IF YOU DON'T ENJOY YOUR WORK, YOU'RE PROBABLY NOT THAT GOOD AT IT ANYWAY.

DO YOU ENJOY HANGING OUT WITH YOUR FRIENDS? IF NOT, DUMP THEM.

I, FOR ONE, DON'T GO TO PARTIES OR DINNER WITH PEOPLE I DON'T REALLY LIKE. THIS MIGHT NOT MAKE OTHERS HAPPY, BUT IT SURE MAKES ME HAPPY.

I SIMPLY WON'T COMPROMISE MY PERSONAL HAPPINESS TO PUT MYSELF IN THE PRESENCE OF PEOPLE I DON'T LIKE.

DON'T LIKE YOUR HOUSE? YOU COULD MOVE OR PAINT IT OR REDECORATE.

DON'T LIKE YOUR CLOTHES? BUY SOMETHING NEW TO WEAR. EVEN IF YOU CAN'T AFFORD EXPENSIVE CLOTHES ...EVEN THE STARS SHOP AT THRIFT STORES!

IN THE END, YOU SHOULD GET ON WITH YOUR LIFE AND LEARN TO ENJOY IT!

THERE ISN'T MUCH TIME LEFT!

WHILE WE'RE AT IT, YOU DON'T HAVE TO BE UNHEALTHY.

YOU CHOOSE, ON SOME LEVEL, EVERY-THING YOU EXPERIENCE IN LIFE...EVEN SICKNESS.

WHEN YOU ARE FULL OF NEGATIVITY AND FRUSTRATION, YOUR BODY REACTS IN NEGATIVE WAYS. YOU DON'T SLEEP WELL. YOU MAY HAVE STOMACH PROBLEMS AND ULCERS. YOU MAY HAVE MIGRAINES.

OF COURSE, NOTHING CONTRIBUTES TO GOOD HEALTH LIKE PROPER DIET AND EXERCISE, BUT MOST PEOPLE ARE TOO STUPID TO ACT ON THIS COMMON KNOWLEDGE.

FRY BUDDY

YOU CAN STOP BEING FAT. IT IS YOUR CHOICE TO EAT THE WAY YOU DO. IT IS YOUR CHOICE TO EXERCISE OR NOT.

GB

GREASY BURGER

THERE ARE ONLY TWO WAYS TO LOSE WEIGHT...

EAT SMARTER AND EXERCISE MORE.

'S GYM

SHAKE

STOP LYING TO YOURSELF AND EVERYONE ELSE. YOU DO NOT HAVE A GLANDULAR PROBLEM.

STOP GOING TO FAST FOOD JOINTS SO OFTEN. THEY MAKE THEIR LIVING SELLING GREASE.

LEAVE THE PARKING SPACES CLOSE TO THE DOOR FOR OLD PEOPLE AND WIMPS.

TAKE YOUR DOG, KID, OR PARTNER FOR WALKS.

GO TO THE GYM.

LET ME ASK YOU...DO YOU LOVE YOUR FAMILY ENOUGH TO GET HEALTHY?

IS THAT CANDY BAR MORE IMPORTANT THAN YOUR KIDS? ARE YOU WILLING TO DIE FOR THOSE FRIES?

HEART DISEASE AND CANCER ARE THE NUMBER ONE AND NUMBER TWO KILLERS IN OUR SOCIETY. YET THEY ARE DISEASES PRIMARILY CHOSEN BECAUSE PEOPLE ARE NOT WILLING TO STOP SMOKING, STOP EATING LIKE PIGS, OR STOP SITTING ON THEIR FAT BUTTS.

CAN YOU REALLY LOOK YOUR FAMILY IN THE EYE AND SAY THAT FETTUCCINE ALFREDO IS MORE IMPORTANT THAN THEY ARE?

DID YOU KNOW THE AVERAGE PERSON SPENDS ABOUT 100 HOURS A YEAR READING. YET THEY SPEND NEARLY 2,000 HOURS IN FRONT OF THE TELEVISION?

FORTY HOURS A WEEK WATCHING TELEVISION BUT ONLY TWO READING?

READING IS A GREAT WAY TO MAKE YOURSELF SMARTER.

IN FACT, I'D RECOMMEND THAT YOU DON'T EVEN HANG AROUND WITH PEOPLE WHO DON'T READ.

HERE ARE A FEW TIPS ON READING BOOKS.

IF AT ALL POSSIBLE, PURCHASE THE BOOK. WHEN YOU ARE INVESTING IN A BOOK THAT HAS LIFE-CHANGING INFORMATION IN IT, YOU NEED TO BUY THE BOOK.

AND BUY LOTS OF BOOKS. KEEP YOUR "TO BE READ" PILE STOCKED.

IF THE BOOK IS YOURS, MARK IT UP. WRITE YOUR NAME IN IT. GET A HIGHLIGHTER AND MARK IMPORTANT PASSAGES.

ONCE YOU'RE DONE WITH THE BOOK, WRITE A SUMMARY OF WHAT YOU LEARNED IN THE FRONT COVER OR ON A BLANK PAGE.

PEOPLE LOVE TO TALK ABOUT HOW STRESSED THEY ARE, DON'T THEY?

MY LIFE IS SO STRESSFUL.

THE HOLIDAYS ARE STRESSFUL.

MY KIDS ARE STRESSING ME OUT.

MY BOSS CAUSES ME SO MUCH STRESS.

THERE ARE EVEN STRESS MANAGEMENT SEMINARS! WHY WOULD YOU WANT TO LEARN HOW TO MANAGE SOMETHING YOU DO NOT NEED AT ALL?

WARNING! OVERWHELMING STRESS WITHIN!

HERE'S A LESSON I LEARNED ABOUT STRESS:

STRESS COMES FROM KNOWING WHAT IS RIGHT AND DOING WHAT IS WRONG.

GET A PEN AND PAPER AND WRITE DOWN SOME THINGS THAT ARE CAUSING YOU STRESS.

CHANCES ARE, YOU KNOW WHAT NEEDS TO BE DONE TO RESOLVE EVERYTHING ON THAT LIST. THE PROBLEM IS, YOU'RE DOING NOTHING OR WHAT YOU'RE DOING IS WRONG.

DO YOU KNOW SOMEONE WHO SAYS MONEY IS OVERRATED OR THAT MONEY IS THE ROOT OF ALL EVIL?

THOSE PEOPLE OBVIOUSLY DON'T HAVE MUCH MONEY!

HAVING MONEY IS A LOT BETTER THAN NOT HAVING MONEY, SO DON'T EVER DIMINISH THE IMPORTANCE OF MONEY OR THE JOY OF HAVING IT.

AW, WHO NEEDS IT...MONEY AIN'T EVERYTHING!

NEW

IF YOU DO, YOU'LL NEVER HAVE MUCH OF IT.

PARDON ME...CAN YOU SPARE SOME CHANGE FOR A GUY WHO'S DOWN ON HIS LUCK?

YOUR ATTITUDE ABOUT MONEY AND ABOUT THE PEOPLE WHO HAVE MONEY HAVE DETERMINED HOW MUCH MONEY YOU HAVE THIS VERY MOMENT.

KEEP IN MIND, THOUGH, YOU DO NOT MAKE MONEY.

YOU EARN IT.

AND IF YOU HAVE A PROBLEM LETTING MONEY GO FROM YOU, THEN YOU WILL HAVE A PROBLEM LETTING MONEY COME TO YOU.

WHEN YOU GET A BILL, PAY IT WITH A SMILE. DON'T GRIPE ABOUT UTILITY BILLS.

HAVE FUN SPENDING YOUR MONEY.

DON'T BE AN IDIOT ABOUT IT, BUT ENJOY IT.

OF COURSE, YOU SHOULD PAY YOUR BILLS AND MEET ALL YOUR OBLIGATIONS FIRST. YOU SHOULD SAVE AND INVEST. YOU SHOULD SHARE.

YOU SHOULD ALSO BE SURE TO HAVE FUN WITH YOUR MONEY.

BUT THINGS COST SO MUCH!

THE PROBLEM ISN'T THAT THINGS COST TOO MUCH. THE PROBLEM IS THAT YOU CAN'T AFFORD THEM.

GRIPING ABOUT HOW MUCH THINGS COST DOES YOU NO GOOD. YOU CAN, HOWEVER, DO SOMETHING ABOUT HOW MUCH MONEY YOU HAVE.

HOW WILL YOU KNOW WHEN YOU HAVE ENOUGH MONEY? YOU CANNOT MEASURE FINANCIAL SUCCESS IN TERMS OF AN AMOUNT. NO AMOUNT IS EVER ENOUGH.

ONLY YOUR BEST EFFORT IS ENOUGH. WHEN YOU HAVE DONE YOUR BEST, BELIEVED YOUR BEST, GIVEN YOUR BEST, AND SERVED YOUR BEST, THEN YOU HAVE RECEIVED THE RIGHT AMOUNT.

FIRST, BELIEVE YOU DESERVE MORE MONEY.

WHEN YOU BELIEVE YOU DESERVE MORE, THEN YOU BEGIN TO GET MORE.

NOW I WANT TO TALK ABOUT RELATIONSHIPS, BUT BEFORE I DO I SHOULD STRESS THAT I'M NO EXPERT.

I HAVE, HOWEVER, READ SOME BOOKS BY SO-CALLED RELATIONSHIP EXPERTS, AND I'VE DETERMINED THEY AREN'T EXPERTS, EITHER.

MANY RELATIONSHIP EXPERTS WILL TELL YOU MEN AND WOMEN ARE DIFFERENT— EVEN FROM DIFFERENT PLANETS!

WE NEED TO REMEMBER WE ARE ALL ALIKE. IT IS THE COMMONALITY THAT WE SHARE THAT WILL BRING US CLOSER, NOT THE DIFFERENCES.

HSSSSS.

ALL RELATIONSHIPS ARE CONSTANTLY CHANGING ORGANISMS. PEOPLE CHANGE, THEREFORE RELATIONSHIPS CHANGE.

CHANGE IS NATURAL.

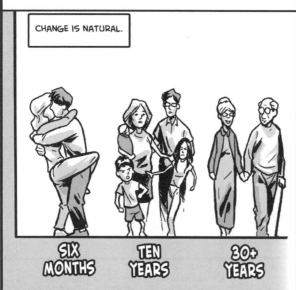

SIX MONTHS

TEN YEARS

30+ YEARS

THE BEST RELATIONSHIPS RENEW THEMSELVES CONSTANTLY. THEY DON'T FOCUS TOO MUCH ON THE FUTURE. THEY DO NOT PUT STOCK IN THE PAST. INSTEAD, THEY FOCUS ON THE NOW.

THEY PUT THEIR ENERGY INTO ENJOYING EVERY SECOND OF WHAT THEY HAVE AT THAT MOMENT.

FAILED MARRIAGE STATISTICS ARE STAGGERING IN THIS COUNTRY. THEY AREN'T SURPRISING, THOUGH.

WE HAVE A SCREWED-UP VIEW OF MARRIAGE THAT PRETTY MUCH DOOMS IT FROM THE START.

MARRIAGE DOESN'T PROVIDE STABILITY. WE'VE ALREADY DETERMINED THAT PEOPLE AND RELATIONSHIPS CHANGE.

MARRIAGE TENDS TO MAKE US TAKE EACH OTHER FOR GRANTED.

BURP!

ACK! ACK!

BRRT!

SKRITCH SKRITCH

MARRIAGE CREATES POSSESSIVENESS.

IT'S MINESESS....

SOME PEOPLE THINK THEIR MARRIAGE LICENSE IS A CERTIFICATE OF OWNERSHIP.

MARRIAGE SIMPLY CANNOT LIVE UP TO THE ROMANTIC MYTH SO MANY PEOPLE CHOOSE TO BELIEVE.

THE MYTH IS THAT MARRIAGE JOINS TWO PEOPLE TOGETHER IN PERFECT HARMONY: TWO HALVES FINALLY UNITED TO MAKE A WHOLE.

WHAT A BUNCH OF HOOEY. TWO PEOPLE ARE BEING JOINED IN THE MYTH THAT IF THEY ONLY HAVE A JOINT CHECKING ACCOUNT AND SHARE A LAST NAME THEY WILL FINALLY BE HAPPY!

BE REALISTIC ABOUT YOUR MARRIAGE. IT'S A CHOICE, NOT AN OBLIGATION. AND IT'S NOT NECESSARILY THE RIGHT CHOICE FOR EVERYONE.

AM I CONDONING LIVING TOGETHER WITHOUT MARRIAGE?

ABSOLUTELY. YOU DON'T KNOW SOMEONE UNTIL YOU DO. IF A LAW WERE PASSED THAT TWO PEOPLE COULD NOT MARRY WITHOUT FIRST LIVING TOGETHER FOR ONE YEAR, THE DIVORCE RATE IN AMERICA WOULD BE CUT IN HALF.

AM I IN SUPPORT OF DIVORCE?

SURE. THERE IS NOTHING WRONG WITH DIVORCE IF IT ENDS A CRUMMY MARRIAGE. IT'S BETTER TO HAVE A GOOD DIVORCE THAN A BAD MARRIAGE

IN ANY RELATIONSHIP, YOU MUST RETAIN YOUR INDIVIDUALITY. GIVE EACH OTHER SPACE. ALLOW SEPARATENESS IN TERMS OF SPACE, INTERESTS, AND FRIENDS.

STAY WHO YOU ARE. DEVELOP YOURSELF AS AN INDIVIDUAL. THE BETTER YOU ARE, THE BETTER THE TWO OF YOU WILL BE.

WE'VE BEEN TOLD OPPOSITES ATTRACT.

THAT'S TRUE WITH MAGNETS, BUT NOT RELATIONSHIPS. OPPOSITES MAY ATTRACT, BUT NOT FOR LONG.

YOU HAVE TO HAVE THINGS IN COMMONS—LOTS OF THINGS—OR YOU'LL TIRE OF EACH OTHER QUICKLY.

AND REMEMBER, YOU DON'T NEED ANYONE.

NEEDY PEOPLE AREN'T ATTRACTIVE. INDEPENDENCE IS ATTRACTIVE.

NO ONE CAN TAKE CARE OF YOU OTHER THAN YOURSELF. YOU ARE RESPONSIBLE FOR YOUR OWN HAPPINESS.

KIDS ARE DIRTY, MESSY, AND EXPENSIVE...

AND THEY ACT THE WAY THEY DO BECAUSE YOU TAUGHT THEM IT'S OKAY TO ACT THAT WAY.

THERE ARE NO BAD LITTLE KIDS. THERE ARE PLENTY OF BAD PARENTS.

YOUR KIDS ARE A DIRECT REFLECTION OF WHAT YOU HAVE TAUGHT THEM. AND JUST LIKE YOU HAVE ALWAYS HEARD, YOUR ACTIONS SPEAK LOUDER THAN YOUR WORDS.

IT IS YOUR RESPONSIBILITY TO SET LIMITS AND BOUNDARIES FOR THE CHILD TO LIVE WITHIN, THEN DISCIPLINE ACCORDINGLY WHEN THEY DO NOT.

BE THE KIND OF PARENT YOUR KID CAN TALK TO, BUT DON'T TRY TO BE THEIR BEST FRIEND.

AND REMEMBER, THEY DO GROW OUT OF IT. PICK YOUR BATTLES, BUT DON'T MAKE EVERYTHING A BATTLE.

PURPLE HAIR GROWS OUT. BAGGY CLOTHES GO OUT OF STYLE. HATS EVENTUALLY TURN AROUND SO THE BILL IS FACING THE RIGHT WAY. KIDS DO BECOME HUMAN AGAIN.

LOVE THEM THROUGH IT.

SEX.

DID THAT GET YOUR ATTENTION?

SEX IS THE COOLEST THING ON THE PLANET, AND SOCIETY HAS DONE ITS BEST TO MAKE IT WRONG AND DIRTY.

SEX IS NOT WRONG. SEX IS VERY RIGHT. WE NEED TO GIVE OURSELVES PERMISSION TO ENJOY IT.

MAKE IT EXCITING. GET CREATIVE.

IF IT FEELS GOOD AND YOU BOTH AGREE TO IT, DO IT! JUST ENJOY EACH OTHER.

AND WHEN IT COMES TO YOUR KIDS, YOU SHOULD TEACH THEM THAT SEX IS NATURAL AND NORMAL. HOWEVER, YOU SHOULD PROVIDE THEM WITH A FOUNDATION OF RESPECT, RESPONSIBILITY, AND SAFETY.

AM I SAYING KIDS SHOULD HAVE SEX? NO.

I'M SAYING THAT KIDS ARE GOING TO HAVE SEX, SO TEACH THEM HOW TO DO IT RESPONSIBLY.

LOVE IS THE KEY TO MANY THINGS.

MOST PEOPLE THINK LOVE JUST APPLIES TO RELATIONSHIPS, BUT IT IS ALL POWERFUL. IT IS THE KEY TO YOUR SUCCESS AND HAPPINESS.

LOVE WHAT YOU DO.

LOVE THOSE YOU DO IT FOR.

LOVE OTHERS.

LOVE YOURSELF.

LOVE IS THE KEY TO BUSINESS SUCCESS, PROSPERITY, AND HAPPINESS.

ONE SECRET TO SUCCESS IS THAT THE MORE YOU GIVE, THE MORE YOU GET.

YOU GET THE WEIGHT YOU WANT BY GIVING UP FOODS THAT ARE BAD FOR YOU.

YOU GET SUCCESS BY GIVING UP ALL THE HABITS THAT KEEP YOU FROM BEING SUCCESSFUL. THINGS LIKE WATCHING TOO MUCH TV, LOUSY WORK HABITS, AND BEING LAZY.

THAT'S HOW YOU GET MONEY, TOO. GIVE SOME OF THE MONEY YOU HAVE. THE MORE YOU GIVE OF WHAT YOU HAVE, THE MORE YOU ACTUALLY GET.

FEED THE CHILDREN. FEED THE HOMELESS. SAVE THE WHALES.

IT IS ONLY WHEN YOU GIVE THINGS AWAY THAT YOU MAKE ROOM FOR MORE...AND ITS USUALLY BETTER STUFF!

GIVING THOSE WHO ACTUALLY NEED WHAT YOU ARE GETTING RID OF— WHETHER ITS MONEY OR AN OLD SOFA—HELPS CREATE THE ABUNDANCE NECESSARY TO REPLACE IT.

NO WAY TO AVOID IT—WORK IS PART OF EVERY-ONE'S LIFE.

WELL, SOME PEOPLE HAVE FOUND A WAY TO AVOID IT, BUT YOU DON'T WANT TO EMULATE THEM.

PLEASE GIVE

WORK IS A SOURCE OF INCOME... AND A SOURCE OF PER-SONAL AND PROFESSIONAL FULFILLMENT AND SATISFACTION.

#$@*!!!

BUT NO MATTER HOW MUCH YOU LOVE WHAT YOU DO, SOMETIMES IT JUST ISN'T MUCH FUN. EVEN IF WHAT YOU DO IS THE TRUE FULFILLMENT OF ALL THE CREATIVE AND FUN ENERGY YOU HAVE IN YOUR HEART, MIND, BODY, AND SOUL, SOMETIMES YOU WILL GET TIRED OF IT AND HATE IT.

THE BEST YOU CAN DO IS LOVE THE PARTS YOU CAN AND JUST SUCK IT UP AND DEAL WITH THE REST.

HERE ARE THREE REASONS TO GO TO WORK EVERY DAY...

TO KEEP EXISTING CUSTOMERS. THEY'RE THE LIFEBLOOD OF ANY BUSINESS, AND YOU SHOULD MAKE SURE THEY KNOW AND LOVE YOU.

TO CREATE NEW CUSTOMERS. YOU WANT TO BRING IN NEW CUSTOMERS, TREAT THEM RIGHT, AND TURN THEM INTO REPEAT CUSTOMERS.

TO MAKE YOURSELF AND YOUR ORGANIZATION THE KIND THAT OTHER PEOPLE WANT TO DO BUSINESS WITH.

THIS IS THE TOUGHER ONE.

TATTOO MONTHLY

TOP ARTIST

THE VALUE AND PERSONALITY OF AN ORGANIZATION IS ONLY A REFLECTION OF THE VALUES AND PERSONALITIES OF THE INDIVIDUAL EMPLOYEES.

HAVE YOU EVER WALKED INTO THE DEPARTMENT OF MOTOR VEHICLES AND IMMEDIATELY THOUGHT, "THIS IS NOT GOING TO BE A PLEASANT EXPERIENCE?" THE ATTITUDE OF THE EMPLOYEES FILLED THE AIR WITH AN OPPRESSIVE FEELING THAT JUST SCREAMED AT YOU.

ALL BUSINESSES SCREAM AT THEIR CUSTOMERS, BUT YOU CAN CONTROL THE MESSAGE.

WHAT DO YOUR CUSTOMERS FEEL ABOUT YOU AND YOUR BUSINESS?

HERE ARE A FEW MORE SHORT LESSONS THAT CAN HELP YOU THROUGH A TOUGH DAY AT WORK:

WHEN YOU WORK, WORK. WHEN YOU PLAY, PLAY. DON'T MIX THE TWO BECAUSE IT ONLY RUINS BOTH OF THEM.

GET THE HARD STUFF OUT OF THE WAY FIRST.

STAY FOCUSED.

WHEN IT QUITS BEING FUN, QUIT. OR FIGURE OUT HOW TO HAVE FUN AGAIN AT WHAT YOU'RE DOING.

AND WHEN IT COMES TO BUSINESS, HERE ARE FEW MORE GOOD RULES FOR THE ROAD...

TREAT PEOPLE BETTER THAN YOU EXPECT TO BE TREATED.

YOU CAN'T GET A GOOD DEAL FROM A BAD GUY.

SIGN HERE.

INITIAL HERE.

AND HERE.

FRIENDS AND FAMILY PAY FULL RETAIL. IF YOU DO GIVE A FRIEND A DISCOUNT, MAKE SURE THEY KNOW THAT BY NOT PAYING FULL PRICE, THEY ARE FORFEITING THEIR RIGHT TO COMPLAIN.

MEET THE AUTHOR

MY LIFE AS A TWIN

AND THE NUMBER ONE, MOST IMPORTANT, GET-THIS-OR-FAIL LESSON FOR BOTH LIFE AND BUSINESS...

DO WHAT YOU SAY YOU ARE GOING TO DO, WHEN YOU SAID YOU WERE GOING TO DO IT, IN THE WAY YOU SAID YOU WERE GOING TO DO IT.

BUT THERE JUST ISN'T ANY TIME TO DO ALL THE THINGS YOU'RE SUGGESTING!

FOR ONCE, I ALMOST AGREE. THERE ISN'T MUCH TIME, AND THERE SEEMS TO BE LESS EVERY DAY.

AND TIME MANAGEMENT IS A JOKE.

TIME CANNOT BE MANAGED. THERE IS NOTHING YOU CAN DO TO GET MORE TIME OR TO STOP TIME FROM MOVING FORWARD.

INSTEAD OF FOCUSING ON TIME, FOCUS ON YOUR PRIORITIES.

OUR PRIORITIES ALMOST ALWAYS GET DONE BECAUSE WE FIND A WAY TO MAKE TIME FOR THE THINGS THAT ARE MOST IMPORTANT TO US.

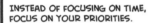

NOTHING STANDS IN THE WAY OF A REAL PRIORITY.

WHAT I'M SAYING IS, THERE IS PLENTY OF TIME TO DO THE THINGS THAT ARE MOST IMPORTANT TO YOU.

IF YOU WANT IT BADLY ENOUGH, YOU'LL FIND TIME FOR IT.

HERE'S A DEFINITION OF SUCCESS BASED ON BALANCE:

SUCCESS IS BEING ALL YOU CAN BE IN EACH AND EVERY AREA OF YOUR LIFE WITHOUT SACRIFICING YOUR ABILITY TO BE ALL YOU CAN BE IN EVERY OTHER AREA OF YOUR LIFE.

DICTIONARY

BE REALISTIC ABOUT BALANCE, THOUGH.

IN ORDER TO ACHIEVE BALANCE, YOU MAY HAVE TO FIRST BECOME UNBALANCED.

IF YOU'RE BROKE AND NEED MONEY, THEN YOU'RE GOING TO HAVE TO BECOME UNBALANCED IN ORDER TO MAKE THAT HAPPEN.

YOU MAY NOT HAVE AS MUCH TIME TO RELAX, PLAY WITH YOUR KIDS, OR HAVE TIME TO YOURSELF WHILE YOU WORK HARD TO EARN MONEY.

GROWTH IN ONE AREA OF YOUR LIFE MAY MEAN LETTING THE OTHERS SLIDE SLIGHTLY.

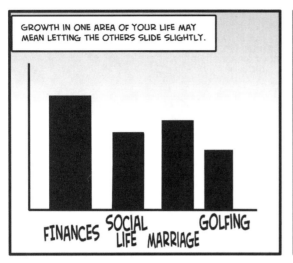

FINANCES SOCIAL LIFE MARRIAGE GOLFING

FOR A WHILE.

NOT FOR LONG THOUGH.

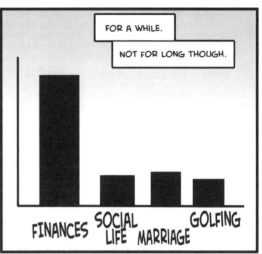

FINANCES SOCIAL LIFE MARRIAGE GOLFING

DO NOT COMPLETELY ABANDON ONE AREA IN PURSUIT OF ANOTHER.

WORK HARD, BUT NOT SO HARD YOU LOSE YOUR LIFE.

PLAY HARD, BUT NOT SO HARD YOU SACRIFICE YOUR LIVELIHOOD.

KLAK

POW

TING

TAP TAP TAP

ABANDON HOPE
'TE WHO ENTER

YOU'VE BEEN TOLD THE VIRTUES OF HOPE YOUR ENTIRE LIFE.

BUT HOPE HAS NEVER DONE YOU A BIT OF GOOD.

HOPE SAYS YOU WISH THAT SOMETHING WILL HAPPEN THE WAY YOU WANT, BUT IT COULD JUST AS EASILY NOT HAPPEN.

HOPE IS GROUNDED IN UNCERTAINTY.

INSTEAD OF HOPE, HAVE FAITH.

FAITH IS GROUNDED IN ABSOLUTE CERTAINTY. FAITH IS KNOWING.

WITHOUT A DOUBT, YOU KNOW SOMETHING IS THERE AND YOU CAN COUNT ON IT.

FAITH GIVES YOU THE COURAGE TO ACT.

WE ALL MAKE MISTAKES.

AND WHEN WE DO, WE FEEL BAD ABOUT IT. THAT'S REGRET, AND IT MEANS WE'RE SORRY AND DON'T WANT TO REPEAT THE SAME ACTION AGAIN.

REGRET IS GOOD.

GUILT, HOWEVER, SERVES NO PURPOSE.

GUILT IMMOBILIZES YOU, AND IT DOESN'T HELP IN ANY WAY.

YOU CANNOT CHANGE WHAT HAS BEEN DONE BY FEELING GUILTY ABOUT IT.

IF YOU MESSED UP, MAKE RESTITUTION AND APOLOGIZE. IF YOU'RE FORGIVEN, MOVE ON.

IF YOU'RE NOT FORGIVEN, MOVE ON ANYWAY.

FORGIVE YOURSELF AND LEARN FROM THE EXPERIENCE.

THERE ARE TWO AREAS OF LIFE.

THOSE YOU CAN CONTROL.

AND THOSE YOU CANNOT CONTROL.

DON'T WORRY ABOUT THE THINGS YOU CAN'T CONTROL. THAT'S STUPID.

THE END IS NEAR

AND IF YOU CAN CONTROL SOMETHING, YOU DON'T NEED TO WORRY. YOU NEED TO ACT.

ZzZZ

YOU CAN'T CONTROL THE PAST AND YOU CAN'T CONTROL THE FUTURE, SO DON'T WASTE TIME WORRYING ABOUT EITHER.

BUT YOU CAN CONTROL THE PRESENT!

YOU'VE BEEN TOLD NOT TO BE SELFISH YOUR ENTIRE LIFE.

BUT THE PEOPLE WHO TOLD YOU THAT WERE DEAD WRONG.

YES, YOU SHOULD SHARE YOUR MONEY AND YOUR STUFF AND YOUR TALENT.

BUT YOU HAVE TO LEARN TO BE SELFISH WITH YOURSELF.

DO NOT DISTURB GENIUS NAPPING

YOUR FIRST OBLIGATION IS TO YOURSELF. YOU CANNOT BE ANY GOOD TO SOMEONE ELSE UNLESS YOU ARE FIRST GOOD TO YOURSELF.

BE SELFISH WITH YOUR TIME.

LEARN TO SAY NO TO THE THINGS YOU DON'T WANT TO DO AND HAVE NO INTEREST IN.

SAY NO TO THINGS THAT KEEP YOU FROM SAYING YES TO WHAT YOU REALLY WANT TO DO IN LIFE.

HAVE YOU EVER HEARD THE OLD SAYING, "A DEAL IS A DEAL?"

WHATEVER HAPPENED TO LIVING UP TO THAT IDEAL?

WE HAVE ALL MADE THE MISTAKE OF OVER PROMISING—YOUR MOUTH OVERLOADS YOUR ASS, AS THE SAYING GOES.

SO? WHAT DIFFERENCE SHOULD THAT MAKE?

YES, IT MIGHT COST YOU TIME OR MONEY TO LIVE UP TO YOUR WORD. IT MIGHT EVEN BE EMBARRASSING OR HUMILIATING.

IF YOU MAKE A PROMISE, KEEP IT. IF YOU SAY YOU ARE GOING TO SHOW UP AT A CERTAIN TIME, BE THERE. IF YOU MESS UP, ADMIT IT AND ACCEPT THE CONSEQUENCES.

ANY LESS MAKES YOU A LIAR.

BUT A DEAL IS A DEAL. MAKE A BETTER DEAL NEXT TIME...BE SMARTER NEXT TIME...BUT THIS TIME LIVE UP TO YOUR COMMITMENT.

45

RICH MAKES UP FOR A LOT OF UGLY.

AND WHY SHOULD I DO ALL THIS STUFF?

BECAUSE YOU CAN! YOU CHANGE, DO BETTER, GET HEALTHIER, AND WORK HARDER BECAUSE YOU CAN!

IF I DO EVERYTHING YOU'RE SUGGESTING, WILL I BE SUCCESSFUL?

YES, I BELIEVE THAT IF YOU TAKE ACTION ON MY SUGGESTIONS, YOU WILL BE MORE SUCCESSFUL.

HERE'S A LITTLE TEST TO HELP YOU DETERMINE IF YOU'VE ACHIEVED SUCCESS. ASK YOURSELF...

AM I HAPPY?

AM I HEALTHY?

AM I LOVING?

AM I LEARNING?

AM I HAVING FUN?

AM I PROSPEROUS?

IF YOU ANSWER YES TO EACH OF THOSE QUESTIONS, THEN CELEBRATE— YOU ARE SUCCESSFUL!

NOW YOU'RE FINISHED WITH THIS BOOK.

BUT ARE YOU REALLY FINISHED?

NOT AT ALL.

NOW IS THE HARD STUFF. NOW YOU HAVE TO TAKE SOME ACTION.

I HOPE YOU WILL TAKE ACTION. I HOPE YOU WILL CHOOSE TO LIVE A DIFFERENT LIFE.

MAYBE FOR YOU IT WILL BE A LITTLE DIFFERENT.

OR MAYBE IT WILL BE DRASTICALLY DIFFERENT.

EITHER WAY, IT TAKES MOVEMENT AND ACTION TO CHANGE.

YOU DON'T HAVE TO DO WHAT I'M SUGGESTING. I DON'T KNOW YOU AND WILL NOT KNOW IF YOU DON'T.

THE END

MY FINAL THOUGHTS

YOU'RE FINISHED!

Wrong! You have only finished the book.

You've looked at a few cool cartoon pictures and read a few words. You may have had a laugh or two and you may have been shocked or angered at something I said. Maybe I even made you think a bit about your life and your situation.

I'm not impressed. All you did was read a comic book so don't pat yourself on the back too quickly.

None of what you just read in this book matters. Even if you gave my words and ideas real consideration and spent hours thinking about your life as a result of reading the book, it wouldn't matter. Why do I say that? Because reading doesn't change things. It's a good start, but it doesn't change things. And thinking about your situation won't change your situation. Action changes things.

That's why I say you aren't finished yet. You are just beginning! Now is where the real work starts. Now is where the real change starts. Because now is the time you decide whether you are going to be one of the many who read and think and then do nothing or one of the few who take action to make their future different from their past.

If you take action on an idea, even just one idea, then I will be impressed. I'm always impressed by action because action is work and work changes results.

So go to work. Get out a pen and a sheet of paper or even write on this very page. Decide what area you are going to attack: your relationships, your financial situation, your job, your health . . . you name it, it's your choice. Then write down the first step you are going to take. Make it tangible by putting pen to paper. This will help you clarify your first step forward. Then put down the pen and start. Don't think about it too much. Just start. Not tomorrow. Not even in a little while. Now!

LARRY WINGET

AUTHOR BIO

Larry Winget is a unique voice in the personal development industry. No one says what he says and no one looks like he looks. He is an original – a one of a kind. He is caustic, straightforward, in-your-face and never minces words. He tells the truth as he sees it and lets the chips fall where they may. He preaches simple concepts of honesty, integrity and personal responsibility and ties those principles to all areas of life and business. And he tops it all off by being hilarious! Rarely do you find someone who can bring solid information that really works delivered in such a refreshing manner and is also funny.

Larry is the author of five New York Times/Wall Street Journal bestsellers. As an award winning professional speaker, he has spoken to nearly 400 of the Fortune 500 companies. He has hosted his own television series, appeared in national television commercials and is a regular on many national news programs. He is a recognized personal development guru to people all over the world in the areas of life, personal finance, parenting and business.

For more information on Larry, please visit his website at **www.larrywinget.com** and join him on twitter and facebook to get his daily rants.

ARTIST BIO

At six years old, **Shane Clester** realized that most people aren't happy with their jobs. Even as he drew robots just to see if he could, he decided at that young age that he would turn his artistic play into work. As Shane grew older and studied the nuances of art, his initial excitement evolved into fascination. He was compelled by the replication of life through seemingly limited tools, and embarked on a quest to learn technical proficiency. In the early 2000s, Shane studied briefly under Jim Garrison, well-known for his art anatomy and technical skills. Shane then relocated from Arizona to California, where he learned a powerful lesson: You have to study to be an artist, and then you have to learn the business of being an artist.

Shane discovered that he needed to sell himself before he could sell a product. Over the course of the next several years, he broadened his portfolio to include youth-oriented art and comic books, and sourced clients by attending conferences and book fairs. Some of his clients have included leading comic book publisher IDW, Hasbro, Scholastic, Macmillan, and Times of London. Shane is currently a staff artist for Writers of the Round Table Inc. Of his many projects, Shane is particularly proud of *Skate Farm: Volume 2*, a graphic novel he produced, *Mi Barrio* based on Robert Renteria's *From the Barrio to the Board Room*, Chris Anderson's *The Long Tail*, and a comic book adaptation of *Art of War*. He is currently working on Marshall Goldsmith's *What Got You Here Won't Get You There*, and an adaptation of Machiavelli's *The Prince*, both for Round Table Comics.

Look for these other titles from SmarterComics and Writers of the Round Table Press:

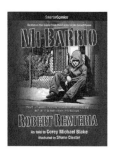

Mi Barrio from SmarterComics
Robert Renteria as told to Corey Michael Blake
Illustrated by Shane Clester

"Don't let where you came from dictate who you are, but let it be part of who you become." These are the words of successful Latino entrepreneur Robert Renteria who started life as an infant sleeping in a dresser drawer. This poignant and often hard-hitting comic memoir traces Robert's life from a childhood of poverty and abuse in one of the poorest areas of East Los Angeles, to his proud emergence as a business owner and civic leader today.

The Art of War from SmarterComics
Sun Tzu Illustrated by Shane Clester

As true today as when it was written, THE ART OF WAR is a 2,500-year-old classic that is required reading in modern business schools. Penned by the ancient Chinese philosopher and military general Sun Tzu, it reveals how to succeed in any conflict. Read this comic version, and cut to the heart of the message!

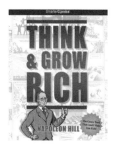

Think and Grow Rich from SmarterComics
Napoleon Hill Illustrated by Bob Byrne

Think and Grow Rich has sold over 30 million copies and is regarded as the greatest wealth-building guide of all time. Read this comic version and cut to the heart of the message! Written at the advice of millionaire Andrew Carnegie, the book summarizes ideas from over 500 rich and successful people on how to achieve your dreams and get rich doing it. You'll learn money-making secrets - not only what to do but how - laid out in simple steps.

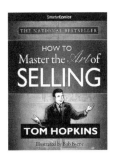

How to Master the Art of Selling from SmarterComics
Tom Hopkins Illustrated by Bob Byrne

With over one million copies sold in it's original version, *How to Master the Art of Selling from SmarterComics* motivates and educates readers to deliver superior sales. After failing during the first six months of his career in sales, Tom Hopkins discovered and applied the very best sales techniques, then earned more than one million dollars in just three years. What turned Tom Hopkins around? The answers are revealed in *How to Master the Art of Selling from SmarterComics*, as Tom explains to readers what the profession of selling is really about and how to succeed beyond their imagination.

Overachievement from SmarterComics
John Eliot, PH.D. Illustrated by Nathan Lueth

In OVERACHIEVEMENT, Dr. Eliot offers the rest of us the counterintuitive and unconventional concepts that have been embraced by the Olympic athletes, business moguls, top surgeons, salesmen, financial experts, and rock stars who have turned to him for performance enhancement advice. To really ratchet up your performance, you'll need to change the way you think about becoming exceptional-and that means truly being an exception, abnormal by the standards of most, and loving it. Eliot will teach you that overachieving means thriving under pressure-welcoming it, enjoying it, and making it work to your advantage.

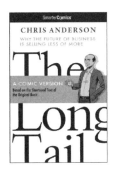

Long Tail from SmarterComics
Chris Anderson Illustrated by Shane Clester

The New York Times bestseller that introduced the business world to a future that's already here. Winner of the Gerald Loeb Award for Best Business Book of the Year. In the most important business book since The Tipping Point, Chris Anderson shows how the future of commerce and culture isn't in hits, the high-volume head of a traditional demand curve, but in what used to be regarded as misses--the endlessly long tail of that same curve.

For more information, please visit www.smartercomics.com

The book that inspired the comic...

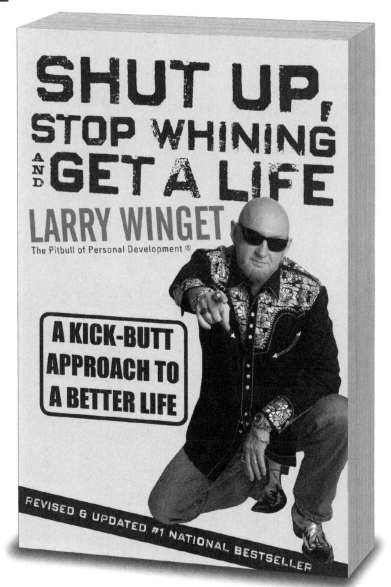

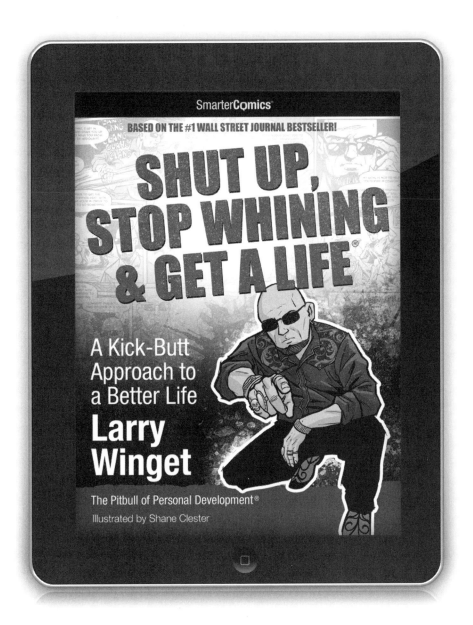

Shut Up, Stop Whining & Get a Life and other SmarterComics™ books
are available for download on the iPad and other devices.

www.smartercomics.com

SmarterComics™

SmarterComics™

www.smartercomics.com